𝔄 𝕳eartstorm

(A window to the soul,
in poetic forms)

Nadina Boun

A Heartstorm

ISBN-13: 978-1467923026

ISBN-10: 1467923028

First Published 2011 by
Nadina Boun

Printed in USA
CreateSpace.

To my muse, my inspiration, my mentor; Life.

To all the women who have loved me, hurt me and inspired me;
To Maya, Diana, Jordana.

TABLE OF CONTENTS

Love lost in the ashes of remembrance

Foreward

A heartstorm is a collection of 68 poems I wrote over the years.
This is a work of more than 12 years of memories, inspired by
love, pain, joys, sorrows, faith and more. This is a collection
giving thanks to all those who have crossed my path, in joy,
sorrow, love, and abandon.

The poems in this book have been rated and selected by three
different people, with different likings, and picked amongst a
pool of many others that may never see the light. Many thanks
to you all for taking the time to critique and read my poetry.

It must be said, that as I matured and learned, so did my style
and my writing, so did my thoughts and my emotions, which
you will find in these pages. I hope you will enjoy reading and
perhaps relate to many of the poems herein.

Nadina.

LOVE LOST IN THE ASHES OF REMEMBRANCE

It was always you

Look not behind you for what is past is gone,
And what was you and I will be no longer now.
Search not for ways to change what was done,
Give no justifications for what remains undone.

The past shall remain but a memory in the brain
And not even the rain shall ever erase your name.
Our passion shall remain but a fire in our heart,
The line of love & hate need not break if we part.

Together we have crossed bridges over distances,
Battles we have fought, to stay by each other's side,
Mountains we have climbed in search of our faith,
And our bond has strengthened through our pains.

Yet it is only the past that dies with a new light,
But grieve not for what is lost in the blindness of night,
What once was, even if buried, will not remain the same,
But think not of what to change, should we be again.

Look through your eyes to see me looking at you,
For the way you look at me is the same as I do you,
Feel your heart burning with longing and sadness,
For I shall not deny mine, its weeping in silence.

Despite what I might say to turn you the other way,
I cannot take away the pain I inject you with today,
But let me not see your eyes as I go my own way,
Attempt not through my weakness to make me stay.

My Siren

A river of sensations flooded my being
When a siren emerged from the dead living,
Sparkles of light and a craving from within me
Revealed themselves like a shadow behind me.

I took the courage to dive so deep
Into the illuminated unknown of the sea,
My siren came to join me unleashed
From the chains that bound her so deep.

Waves crushed against our bodies united,
Sharks attacked with their teeth uninvited,
Creatures of the sea harassed us repeatedly,
And the flow of the sea turned deadly.

Patience kept us holding on to the weeds,
Unity gave birth between us to new seeds,
Passion ignited our bodies into one,
Come what may we swore to remain.

And under the dark blue my siren fed me,
Against cold warmed me and close held me,
When suffocated mouth to mouth breathed me,
From sea mysteries her tail surrounded me,

Then suddenly the dream disappeared, passed,
And waves threw us into divided paths,
Tears we shed made of the sea an ocean,
Her tail was to another bound in motion.

My heart shredded into pieces, burst out,
Its parts bleeding lost into the ocean,

And my body sunk into the green depth,
Where upon it sea creatures fed.

Blood gushed out of my veins, my lungs,
Waves were talking in different tongues,
I was unsure if my siren abandoned me,
I was unaware she has betrayed me.

And though our hearts were locked together,
Only her memory will remain forever,
For she has stepped over a great distance
Far ahead and beyond my resistance.

Was she still alive, was she dead?
To this mystery no answers were shed.
I had lost her and all hope,
My princess of the sea my only one.

Don't let go

I see the pain in your eyes
And I wish I can take it away,
I see the worries on your frown
And I wish I can erase them away.

I look in your mirror and it screams;
You feel empty, alone, bordering tears,

You walk, you talk, you smile in pretense,
Upon the slightest word you act in defense,

You put on a cold, uncaring face,
When you crave is a warm embrace,

You may lie, you may hide, even run away,
But the truth in your eyes reveals it anyways.

I am here today, gone tomorrow,
No intention to cause you any sorrow,
My eyes adore you if only you know,
My heart breaks if you let yourself go.

Had I known

Had I known
it was the last time I would see the sun
I would have bathed
naked under its warming rays,
I would have squinted
hard to see it shining high.

Had I known
I was never to see the sky again,
I would have looked
more intently at the clouds,
In what shape they came,
in what language they spoke.

Had I known
the last time had passed to see you,
I would have stared
deeply into your blue expressive eyes,
Memorized every line on your face,
every trace of your smile.

Had I known
it was the last time we were ever to speak,
I would have weighed
the words slipping from my tongue,
I would have showed you without words
how deep your love has grown.

I would have whispered in your ears
echoes of kisses long gone,
I would have melted in your eyes
one last time before dawn,

I would have smiled despite myself
as I watched you leave.

Fantasy sail

It is fantasy in the realm of reality,
a step to the unknown,
perhaps the forbidden,
a path leading to nowhere,
but an intriguing adventure,
riding on the waves of the sea,
dangerously alluring.

Sailing,
in search of an unknown territory
will the quest be met,
is a question yet to be answered.

Like following the sound of a tune
that is only ringing in your head,
making love blindfolded,
being led with nothing but emotions,
it is like having faith,
and being guided by the unseen;
a step towards the unknown
realm of fantasy and illusion,
where reality might meet ,
if only in dreams.

Will the tide overtake the journey,
leading the ship astray,
or will the sailor awaken,
from the sea's embracing motion,
and search for yet another day?

Drunk on you

Drunk on your words
in this ocean of desire,
Let the night engulf us
with its melody or fire,

Entranced you lift me high
as I soar on the wings of love
eternal,
But then you mellow me down,
I dive into your sea of love
Infernal,

Taking me to places
if only in my mind,
where lost and hypnotized
I become blind,

And like waves of the ocean
you carry me so far, forever more,
in a sweet melodic embrace
that moves all of me to the core,

My passion reignited,
my desire burns again,
to you I long to soar,
lose it all,
with no words to explain.

Pleasurable pain
you instill in me
pulling me to you
like a magnetic field,

holding back
from this tension so near,
like a dance of souls
that only our eyes can see,

and as the tension subsides
another wave hits me,
I crash on its shore
Willingly.

Entranced and hypnotized
it captivates all of me,
in this dreamy state
you leave me for a while,
with an increasing desire,

My need is in longing
for more of this art,
Submissive and weak
a dream plays itself
within my mind,

You rob my soul from its state
leaving me breathless
my heart in wait,

yearning is my body
with an insatiable fire
calm like the sea
you pull me towards
your danger so sweet,

with a shift of tunes and colors
you hold me down stronger
Lost in the sea of love

drunk on its fire longer.

Another love song

If we stay
love threatens to slowly fade away
if we part,
there's no guarantee we'll see the day,

I know the pain you feel;
a pain of loss anyway
I know the wounds are deep,
getting sharper by the day.

Forgive and forget,
is what people often say
yet familiar am I
to pain that opts to stay,

Nothing is yet broken
though scarred we remain.
Should love be set free
to by itself return,
or will the absence make it
vanish and burn?

You make a choice,
then you grieve the loss,
but tell me have we gained,
anything but loss?

Is there a balance for love to grow,
or are we chasing ghosts in the snow,
is there room for love to be
across the years,
or is the wait too strong

21

to leave us in tears,

is love just a glimpse
of what is inside us real,
or are we buying ourselves
more time to steal,

and what is it we take,
but a little from each other
though the feeling is strong,
in memory is the other,

will the distance show us
who we are to one another,
or will we open our eyes
to a new day, a new lover,

is love what keeps us alive,
giving life to life,
or is death our only hope
to be reborn to life?

Sweet little angel

A sweet little angel as thou art
let the mountains roll with thy smile,
whisper to the wind for a while,
thy soul from mine shall not depart.

Thine shining eyes on thy enticing face
hold my heart in an eternal embrace,
as stars twinkle in lasting night,
so doth thy smile in absence of light.

My beloved angel descending from the sky
fly above the rivers like a butterfly,
and when the waters shall cease to be,
with thy breath revive their energy.

Thou shalt make the birds sing
and grow wiser under thy wing,
pray and worship thee, as mine
eyes that see thee so divine.

Thou bring'st out the sun thru the clouds,
and she, with thy powers, hath no bounds,
thine whispers soothe mine sorrows,
and from thy sun, love I borrow.

Thou art my unseen happiness,
with thee, mine misery and anger are less,
thou art my immortal angel of heaven,
for thou art a diamond amongst all men.

Say goodbye

I've never been as afraid as I am today;
Of losing you forever there is no hideaway.
If I stay, I can feel her in your mind
If I run, she threatens to take your heart.

Surely I must understand, ironic as it is,
Your desire for her growing deep within,
And I must try to bring you back to me,
Though at heart I know you no longer need me.

The love you speak of is but a memory now,
Even the lust we had seems gone somehow,
We are back to playing games
though things are no longer the same.

And it sickens me to be in your arms,
when it's her who is turning you on
and it hurts when you say you love me,
when it's her face you ache to see.

Disguise

What is love
            but a limitless energy that binds us together?
And what is passion
                        but an overflowing desire of love?
What is grief
                        but a lost or unattained happiness?
And what is pain
                        but shattered expectations and dreams?

What is friendship
                        but a silent talk of the mind?
And what is emotion
                        but an apparent motion of the soul?
What is mother earth
                        but a boundless reproductive womb?
And what is the sky
                        but an infinite painting in disguise?

And what is me without you
                        but a mold broken in two
And what is me without you
                        but un-fulfillment of us two
For it is your energy enter-twined
                        with mine that makes us one
And it is your ongoing love
                        that feeds my passion, and mine your love

And it is your grief
                        that makes my happiness
And it is your pain
                        that builds my dreams
And between the earth and sky

You become my womb in disguise.

Reflection in the water

The salty waters enrapture me
with their melody,
As they come crashing to my feet, gently

The sound of the breaking waves
Brings me back to a forgotten landscape;
Their foamy shape generating afar,
Engulfs me in a memory far behind.

The gutsy breeze seduces my skin,
As it gently pinches me with a thrill,
The grainy debris in my grip,
Dissolve suddenly, between my fingers slip.

And I bend down and draw a line
On their golden texture so fine.

Thunder illuminates the sky in a flash,
Rendering my senses for an instant, numb;

An image described in the foggy clouds,
Takes me back to a time that once was,
And all through the night I sat entranced
By the drizzling skies on my hands.

Weeping in silence without tears,
For rain and wind I could not hear,

And the picture above painted in black
Stretched wider in a melodic track,
That took me back to that one special tune
When you and me danced under the moon.

Lost notes

Every time he looks to the west
And sees a pigeon without its nest,
On a rooftop perched, silent and still,
He remembers his beloved still,

Wishing to send her his words of love,
But to his agonies she has no heart,
Letters he writes but does not part,
From these words on papers he scribed.

For in his longing the pigeon remained,
As if to remind him again of his pain;
Like him, silent and still she stands alone,
Whispering afar, words only to him known,

As a tear gently sheds itself from his eye,
His heart once more begins to cry.

And in his sadness, she could still deny,
The love he bears her, in a distant sigh
That speaks of hearts not to be bound,
In the stillness where he is now found.

And a parchment he takes and unfolds,
The words he had written in ten folds,
And to his chest crumbles the notes,
That echo in his heart without tones.

And flies away the pigeon, so high,
A scream escapes his lips in Ah
As her wings flutter towards the far
Blue horizon that bears no star.

On his beloved's page, he then tries,
with deep regret, to close his eyes.

Lament

Oh my sadness, oh my longing,
My grief and silent suffering
Had I known of this bitter ending
Of the pain that keeps on growing.

Oh sweet misery that crept upon me,
Oh thorns so deep twisting inside me,
Had I known the crime I would suffer
Would eternally come to haunt me.

Oh deceitful and alluring eyes,
Oh see how my heart now cries,
Oh what hurtful words to say,
Oh what price to have to pay.

Had I known of my recent demise,
Had I known of that sour prize,
Oh what grief can silence this wound,
Oh how sadness weighs in its womb.

Oh my pride to bear this offense,
In voiceless tongues not even protest,
Oh how a heart can be so cruel,
Had I known it would be you.

Fly

She loved you like none,
to adoration,
hated you
to the point of death,

and the calm that remained
in this fluctuation,
brought nothing but pain
in its breadth.

So let this butterfly
now silently fly,
forever away
from your captivating eyes,

but to one flower
she's eternally bound,
its honeydew the sweetest
she has yet found.

And though she wishes to rest her wings,
once and again on its petals so wide,

its pollen blinds her
in a confused tide,
and its thorns squeeze her
with their stings.

So let this butterfly forever be lost,
from this garden she so once adored,

for if she remains she will be but torn,

between her freedom and the love of a rose.

Longing

As I turn the pages and seasons drift away
I find myself thinking of you once again.
The aching has left me, healed by the pain,
But faded and untraceable, the memory still remains.

And the longing I feel seems to never end,
For despite the hope, we might have seen the end,
And here I lay again, silently whispering your name,
As my dreams lift me high to see your face.

And as I awaken, I cannot truly tell,
how touching you feels, for in longing I still dwell.

I wonder, should the distance blind my eyes,
And in your absence my heart forget its cries,
Or should you remain engraved forever on a stone,
That has become my soul after you were gone.

Should I simply forget the inconceivable days,
Whence your smile on my past shed beautiful rays?
Oh I cannot dare to remember, yet I cannot bear to forget,
In my longing for you, I surrender with each sun that sets.

A vision, a warning

Days drift by as she sits on the shore,
Remembering a time with the waves drifting ashore,

In a tranquil sea ahead, she hails a scream aloud,
For the ship she still seeks, left far behind,

The clouds now rising in gray and blue,
Witnessed the sinking of the aboard crew,

But here she waits for her captain alone,
Praying the waves to deliver his bones.

And as the sun sets high, blindingly warm,
She opens her eyes to a ship that is torn,

Reaching from afar, she calls out a name,
But the image disappears, in the sea, untamed.

Daybreak draws near, she awakens from the dream,
On her cheek a tear, a warning of the unseen.

Colours

In the space of a lifetime
Where fantasy and reality meet,
You have come to mark a time
Where future and past could meet.

In the glimpse of a passing day
When often we are led astray,
You have entered through a door
That my heart could not ignore.

In a blink of a flickering eye
Where every second is a lost time,
You have poured on me a light
That will forever shine bright.

In a momentary lapse of joy
Where life and love as one join,
You have left an imprint inside me
That will trace itself in my memory.

In a vanishing moment in time
When lost, we sink in the great divide,
You have come to renew my flight
With your breath of colourful delights.

The castle

A tingling voice echoes in the distance
Arousing my senses, numb in resistance,

A twinkling portrait of a beloved dame,
Across the blazing fire, rises in a flame,

Embellished in the whisper of the breeze,
That raptures my soul, humming in my ears,

A warrior of hearts, I've laid down my arms,
The fight I have lost, my sword cast aside,

In praise I have failed to capture her charms,
I chase from my castle her shadow by my side.

I guess I've never loved you

It just dawned on me now suddenly;
I guess I don't love you, oh baby,

I revel in the feelings I had with you
Longing for the passion I saw in you,

We're worlds apart and I barely know you,
Closed is my heart and I fight loving you,

I long for the feeling, maybe in another's arms,
Let go the memory of what I thought was love,

I guess I never loved you but ached to have you,
A selfish desire within to again experience you,

I guess I longed for arms to hold me with passion,
Your face in my memory, was one I imagined,

I guess I lied about forever loving you,
Passion, lust and longing are what I missed about you,

But love among these is just the longing to have you,
seems I've never loved you like I told you.

Point of no return

So we stand at the point of no return
confused, yet still the flames do burn,
and in sadness we are meant to break,
though our emotions are still awake.

But the roads we travel cross only once;
I lie awake yet like one deceased,
For clouds in my head have eased,
The Blood in my veins turned still.

I know not what to think, nor how I feel,
I wish you away, yet I want you here,
Words echo in emptiness when we speak,
For when we are together we are weak.

We forgive but not forget the pain,
In our thoughts, point a finger to blame,
We play pretend and wish it would last,
With people around, we are another cast.

So we stand again at the point of no return,
in our eyes a farewell, though ashes still burn,
and before our hearts weaken, we take a turn,
farewell this time forever, how quickly love burns!

Your sting

Ask me how or remain indifferent,
The answer you will find is no different
Than every breath I take in your name,
And every word I say in a prayer.

Your blood inside me is intoxicating,
Every breath and every word, captivating,

Your language to my ear is liberating,
poetry in words, in my head ringing.

I drift away on a sea of dreams,
Where the sky above floats with clouds,
Stretching far into extended arms,
Where you and me secretly meet.

I drift away on a sea of desire,
The flames around me rising higher,
And as I drown in a sleepless night,
your blood inside me blazing alight,

Churning and turning I cannot sleep,
Your taste on my lips stings so deep.

Bedroom eyes

You've got those bedroom eyes that hypnotize
And that intoxicating smell to paralyze,

A Heat that beckons an unrestrained passion
With a touch that brings forth sighs of pleasure,

You've got those wild eyes seducing my weakness
Those shivering lips tasting sweet bliss,

A breath of warmth on my body aching in need
As you brush my skin tingling my senses with greed,

How I long to melt within your touch of smooth caresses
And heave in want once your weight on mine presses,

Alas the day is dawning and my mistress awaits
To her I run to satisfy the burning desire that aches.

Fly away

Blinded by your light or is it your darkness,
that once was a heavenly sphere of desire,
down I fell into hell and oblivion,
gasping for air and aching from pain,
as the thread around my neck tightened.

Into the shadows your heart retreated,
leaving me with the image that was once you;
Forgiveness is not a plea you recognize anymore,
for the love inside you extinguished its glow,
and within the remaining cinders of your fire,
you cast away my heart to burn in its desire.

I fear the day to see you again and will I ever?
yet I long for it again despite the pain it creates.
Deep down I fell as you let go my hand from above
and as I squirm in silence in this muddy terrain,
from your obsession I hope to free myself again.

Yet it seems only you can set me free and chain me again
and with this dilemma I am yet faced once again;
my mind is weaker than my heart that breaks,
and the distance does not melt my fire away,
yet with every passing day as I seem to forget,
your memory surges back into my head.

But here I will remain should you lose your way,
and into my arms I will steal you away,
if only in my dreams that hold no tomorrow,
for you will always be my pleasurable sorrow.

Flames of passion

In a blink of an eye
you caught my smile
And shining in your eyes
was a light so bright,

In a glimpse of a morning dew
Heaven and earth collided
When your eyes in mine melted
And reality in fantasy withdrew,

In a moment of total abandon
My dream in yours grew,
And from your lips a new flavor
Stole my other visions too,

In an instant of surrender
You and I both knew
That heaven on earth can be true,
But our hearts could not defend it,

In a sudden eclipse of passion
When my heart upon you crashed,
The dream I had suddenly vanished
And lost I remained in its ashes,

In a moment of defeat,
Will you save me from this turn,
Where my soul runs to burn
In the flames of its heat?

The dying rose

The dying rose of my beloved,
The dark kiss of my angel,
Like dried blood in my veins,
Like a black hole in my soul,
Shall forever dwell in my heart,
Shall but a faint memory remain
'Til the day she awakens me again,
From my dying slumber in wait.

In longing I shall die as I await,
With her cold heart upon me,
With her cold lips on my face
Like a dying bride in a garden of roses,
She revives me from this slumber
In which I sink so deep,
Into her arms in a dark embrace,
She restores my love.

The shadow of her fears surround me,
Where the sun sets on a new day,
Into the night she captures me,
In a silent and deadly embrace.

My garden of Eden perishes
in her dark light like faded flowers,
A tarnished painting of my princess
Where her name bears no face,
In a stained bed of blood I lay
Vanquished by the sun of day,
By the withering beauty of my queen.

When night falls

And when night falls down over the land
and darkness covers all in shades of gray,
the streets I cross still speak your name,
of a time when we danced, hand in hand,

As lights go out in this stretching city
and the sky sheds its velvety black veil,
the wind whispers your name in a melody,
that takes me back to those nights in wait.

In longing, in aching, I awaited your embrace,
sighing and yielding I surrendered to your taste,
waking and dreaming, I yearned to touch you again,
falling and weakening, I faded to with you remain.

As night came down, slowly over our heads,
the messages of love I sent, were drowning ahead,
as you left my hand with a promise for the morrow,
the wind carried my songs to ends with no tomorrow.

As night falls again, and across your face I see,
I try to close my eyes, to escape the pain I feel,
and hiding in the shadows of a far away distant tree,
I cover my ears to silence your voice that echoes to me.

As darkness engulfs the city, its blackness over the streets,
I rush seeking shelter and cover my body under the sheets.
Through the whispers of the night where shadows disappear,
the thought of you brings shivers to make you seem so real.

Stretching void

A void is stretching, inside me spreading,
Its emptiness around me increasingly growing.
Engulfed by this immensity, terribly haunting,
My heart bursts out, screaming in longing.

A void you have left, within these closing walls;
Their grip around me tightens with sharpened claws,
Insufferable and cold is this empty space,
Without your warmth to give it a face.

Swept by the wind of forgetfulness, slapping my face,
Cast in the shadows of yesterdays, without a trace,
It seems I am fading in a faceless, aging time,
The void stretching deep, under this skin of mine.

Solitude has reigned where your love once grew,
Accumulating memories of the days we once knew,
An emptiness is stretching, on the surface it crawls,
Alluring is your memory in this void that grows.

Immortal

Immortal is your memory,
A fetus inside my brain,
A painful killer is your absence,
A tumor within my days.

A window within my frame breaks
As your ray of light penetrates,
Walls crumble in this space,
As your love all else invades.

Immortal is your presence here,
Your imprints conquer my fear,
But dead is the hope that remains,
And immortal shall remain a name.

A vampire's kiss 2

One vampire's thought crept upon me at night,
as the sting of her kiss burned deeply on my neck,
I heard her whisper my name, felt her breath upon me,
My body shivered in ache, hungry for her to feed on me.

She left me in this state, with but a kiss of her lips,
longing and in need, in wait for yet a another sting,
the touch of her caress still burns on my skin,
as I shiver in wait, for her to take me again.

The night is dark, enveloping me with its veil,
but oh where is my mistress, oh come do not fail.

My longing is burning, my desire feeds my flame,
as I gaze at my mistress, and she doth me the same.
Without warning, she takes me away,
and drunk from her lips, I remain.

A single kiss cannot suffice, to sustain my hunger,
yet I crave it with much desire, and feel it even stronger,
for within her lips my blood she drains,
taking with but a kiss, all of me just the same.

I shiver and I moan, crying for more of this sweet pain,
and yet she leaves me in want, as much as she leaves me
drained.

And as you read those words I speak,
words I steal from your lips to make them real,
I shall come again my love, if only to steal you again.

Burning your love

I see your love suffers
                the absence of my affection,
when no matter what I say,
                I cannot spare your affliction.
My eyes are betrayed by my heart deceived,
the love inside is still, after it's been conceived.

The canvas in my mind has a painted smudge,
of its entirety I am unable to judge.
I drag you with my doubts, in this hellish flame,
watch you burn in silence, feeling your pain.

I lift you with words and hopes
                to cling to tomorrow,
smashing your dreams between
                disappointment and sorrow.
Wings of joy, your love has quickly acquired,
wrapped on a torching flame of my desire,

blinded by my fire, mistaken for light,
your love gave itself to me as a sacrifice;
I watched its feathers scorch and burn,
your heart screaming, in muffled burns.

Torn apart, I watch your heart in parts divided,
my spear deep in its wounds, enflamed, driven,
tearing the flesh apart, etching a hole within,
where ashes of pain and suffering remain .

Cruel pain

Cruel is the pain of today,
sweet it is compared to tomorrow's,
absence can mend the hearts broken,
silence can heal the words spoken.

I will push you away but can you hate me,
and it's a risk I take to lessen your pain,
I am cold and cruel to a love so pure,
maybe you'll turn away,
maybe you'll find a cure.

If your eyes cannot see,
nor your ears my voice hear,
if your heart cannot feel
my warmth or cold near,
if your mind sits still,
freed from my memory,
perhaps time will be kind
to take the pain off your mind.

I did not want to hurt you
but broken I left you,
I do not want to break
whatever strength remains.

hate me if you must,
but do not dwell in this dust;
the love we have will not rust,
but in what may come we have no trust.

In losing you, I am prepared,
but in hurting you more, I am scared,

I let you go in a silent goodbye,
I can hear you still even as you cry.

Betrayal

I can always pretend not to care what you do,
But when alone, my thoughts drift towards you,
And as much as I try to find one other than you ,
My interest disappears when I think of you.

And no matter how far I run to forget,
When I see you again, this I regret,
The charm of your eyes makes me stay,
The lust for you makes me come again.

Fool for your loving, will I remain the same,
Though my feelings have already changed?

I am looking for a way out, still in doubt,
For the doors that I seek, are closed about,
But out a window my heart soon will fly,
For you are not the queen to wear its crown.

The lost queen

Let it be known
If it is still unbeknownst to you,
You are no different than those around you;
You have been picked amongst many to be a jewel
In a castle once governed by a fool,

But you renounced your title
and refused your throne,
And tossed away your crown
to burdens so far borne,

You were chosen to rule
with passion and power,
Yet you chose to be a slave
to external powers,

You were loved,
worshiped and adored,
But soon the new challenge
made you bored,

And here the kingdom remains
chaotic without its queen,
Alas she is now in a comatose,
indifferent and unseen.

Short praise

What beauty emanates
from your eyes so deep,
how soothing is your voice
when u whisper or speak,

you have captured my heart
with melodies so sweet,
I am forever yours
in love, in thought, in deed.

My heart cannot contain
the desires it feels,
you dwell in my mind,
the hours you steal,

I awake and sleep
with your name on my lips,
I ache in wakefulness,
in dreams for your kiss.

Spoken

A bird perched on a tree
chirped gently in my direction,
humming and fluttering,
calling for my attention,

I heard a soft whispering
in between its twittering,
or was it the gentle breeze
carrying a song to my ears?

I called out my beloved's name
and the bird replied just the same,
was it an echo to my voice I wondered
or was it the words my love has spoken?

Show me part 2

She said show me, I am tired of you telling me
Let me feel the warmth you speak of incessantly,

Let me see the spark illuminating in your eyes
When they look at me, for a moment locked in my eyes,

She said show me how much you love me
For words, I've had enough but they couldn't show me,

Let your kindness pour forth, even if deep down it hurts,
Let your love be known, even if tears accompany its burst

She said hold me tight and do not fear the night,
Show me that you love me, give all with delight,

Pour your love upon me, understand but do not judge me,
Give your soul to me, surrender but learn to trust me.

My love

Dancing sparkles in your eye,
make my heart leap out,
In your smile, glittering jewels,
turn my soul alight,

And morning or night,
as long as you're in my sight
No troubles, no pain,
can take away my heart's delight,

As long as in your eyes
I breathe a breath of summer's night,
Vain is my love,
if I cannot love you more with every daylight.

Oh how cruel is the time
to let the past so quickly travel,
Love, oh my love,
I don't have much to offer or unravel,

Keys to that chest, you hold
in your breast, and will never die,
How wonderful does the sun
sparkle its rays in your eyes!

Behold your smile,
a reflection of my soul's pleasure,
Dreams fade, my longing stops,
as I stare at this treasure.

Aye how rude am I to reveal
my burning sensation and desire,

Yearning but appeased
by a look of which they never tire.

A million roses

A million roses will never be as fair,
For in your eyes a beauty hard to bear
Sheds its warmth around a cold night,
And spreads its love to a higher flight.

A million jewels can never compare
To a heart that is pure and very rare,
For through your sweetness shines the night,
And shivers of kindness bring forth delight.

A million suns will never shine as bright,
When your eyes twinkle with a smile, alight
Nor will the moon be as charming a crescent,
When your smooth lips curve in words so pleasant.

In you

In the canvas of your eyes,
I saw a painting of the sky,
A glimmer of a distant star,
somewhere in the night.

In the sweetness of your lips,
I tasted the drink of life;
The richness of all the fruits
of the earth combined.

In the landscape of your skin,
I smelled the many scents
Of incense, flowers and rain,
I sensed the shape of a shapeless
monument that doesn't age.

In the vastness of your heart,
I lost myself to love,
A freedom beyond poetry or words,
Where your eyes in mine fill in the verbs.

Once again

On a forbidden path I still tread,
In your eyes I find a thread
Linking me to those feelings I first felt,
When in your arms I was warmly held.

As I long to hold you before you leave
And press my nose against your neck,
Aching to smell your hair, melt in your chest,
Inhale your perfume as your body heaves,

I stand away and avoid your eyes,
Dying to get a glimpse of your smile,
Hiding my feelings as you look at me
Unable to reveal, what you mustn't see.

But like a bird you have left your nest
Cradled by a heart where you still dwell,
An eternal presence like a candle lit,
Echoing in every beat off my chest.

Angered Heart

In my selfishness I couldn't see,
the face I wanted to smile at me
hid a heart full of pain and grief,
behind eyes lost seeking relief.

In my selfishness I asked for more,
blinded by the many desires I bore,
that weighed on one already broken
by many burdens constantly torn.

In my blindness I pursued the truth,
unwilling to listen, seeking more proof,
tearing a heart wandering aimlessly,
its face before me hiding constantly.

In my selfishness, blinded I became
robbing away the joys of today,
burning to ashes a love that was,
now poisoned by an angered heart.

The promise

Let not your heart be an instant saddened
If I depart from you today,

Let not your mind be with confusion laden
For we shall meet another day.

Let not the present destroy the dream,
Let not the distance turn cold the heat,

If we remain all would be in vain,
Parting in silence is our only gain.

For fighting and resistance to this day
have robbed our joys in many ways,

And what remains of that vision ahead
Is only possible if we break instead.

Hold on to me even when I'm gone,
Run towards me, it won't take long,

Call out my name in the far distance,
One day we'll meet without resistance.

Hold on to the dream, it's never too late,
Hold on to the promise, it won't delay.

CHAINED IN THE PAIN OF DELIVERANCE

Silent peace

Many journeys my soul had undertaken,
its quest to be forgiven or to be forsaken,

and from many promises that had been broken,
remained a phrase to be spoken
of what whence was and never to be,
but in quotes and rhymes for time to see;

a sonnet or a prose or a gothic mystery,
a ballad or a praise or a poem to be...

At times silence is all the soul needs;
a journey of dreams to sounds and peace,

to simply gaze at the sky,
at the clouds forming high,
feel the breeze on your skin,
watch trees play with the wind,
listen to murmurs of nature humming,
droplets of rain against the silence dribbling,

sometimes all the soul needs ,
is a little peace of the mind,

the sky in itself is a colorful painting in disguise,
there's just so much to grasp for the eye.

Hopeless

The strength escapes me
my passion is dormant,
the will stands un-nurtured
the heart remains silent.

Of many trials failed,
of many efforts waved,
of many desires condemned,
hope is fleeting like a trend.

The reason beckons proof,
the feeling hunts deceit,
the vision is stronger still
and what is cannot be conceived.

I lack the words of splendor,
metaphors of the unknown,
I struggle with old ways
scant in present days.

The memory is weakened
the hand is restrained,
the soul breaks free
from illusions and dreams.

Every so oft the tide rises,
waves upon the soul rush,
the door slides open, ajar
and shut again as the tide recedes.

My steps are rooted where I lay,
to move forth in this foggy terrain,
engraved by fear sinking in mud,
I opt to dwell in what could have been.

Despair

It is bitterness that turns one evil
When innocence is lost
When hope is gone
When to life there is no more reason

From within the fury will emerge
The rage that was once forgotten
And to the deep pain, inside abandoned
The unchained soul will now surrender

It is regret and not sorrow
That transforms life to become hollow
And without the hope of a tomorrow
Life becomes death in a dangerous shadow

It is weakness that calls upon the dead
When the soul has become weary
And a terrible silence will fall
When the hero inside has moved ahead

Chained

Once again I find myself chained
Looking for a release in every way,
In constant search of my sanctuary,
Of a glimmer of light head away.

In solitude I have shunned away,
From my kindred tried to escape;
Traces of kindness I have scraped
And buried emotions in hide away.

In drugs I have been led astray,
Hands bleeding from lack of pain,
The high drifting the feel outside,
My senses betrayed from the inside.

In poetry wanting to share my pain
Tools out of words I have made,
Until pictures inside my mind
Have to reality turned me blind.

Images I have tried to regenerate
In attempt to create my own,
Though my imagination had grown
My hand was unable to illustrate.

War I waged against my other self
The stronger and the weaker apart,
Until grief consumed the better self
And weaker had become my heart.

I sacrificed my wounds to God,
My prayers rose higher and louder,
Still no answer came from above

Until faith became shaken stronger.

I have tempted the devil in exchange
Treated on his path in constant rage,
And through summoned from the depth
He remained in slumber unchanged.

Once again I find myself chained,
Searching for yet another passage,
Knowing not what to carry for luggage
On this new road untamed.

The mask of death

He looked in the mirror, in search of his identity,
At a shell getting disfigured, unable to breathe,
The shadow of a soul aching in desperation,
hovered over his face, through his reflection:

A mask trying to hide inner weakness,
A face trying to deter from ugliness,
A heart longing for the unknown,
An escape from isolation and the known.

A heart searching for love and beauty,
yet a beast clinging to demonic misery.

Under this courageous cover, lies a child crying,
Beaten and defeated from fighting,
His own battles he has lost in humiliation,
Confused and unarmed he gave in to hopelessness.

And beneath his gentle façade ,
the mask of darkness was lurking,
Its pain seductively alluring.
Desperate attempts to regain strength
have left him beaten, sinking in darkness.

Sadness made his eyes look dimmer,
His skin though young, seemed to wither,
He looked weary and pale as death,
His hollow eyes fading in their depth.

Unnoticed had become his presence,
King of nothing, to whom all was meaningless,
He wandered, seeking in life meaning,
with despair by his side, always bleeding.

He tried to wear a smile to the unknown faces,
A simple music for them to draw near,
Perhaps he would find of himself traces
Or find the clue to some lost dream.

The dead were deaf to his approach,
The living were blinded by fears,
And his only comfort in this deception,
Was the open arms of self-destruction.

Victim

Drifting into the unknown
with only visions of chaos and turmoil ahead,
Wanting to cease time from elapsing
and unable to travel back in my own history,

Wishing the earth would stop its motion
yet unable to move freely about it,
Still I remain where I have started,
With nothing to come and nothing to gain,

Chained to what I have become,
Drawn to things I've tasted and seen,
Lost in the vast emptiness that holds me captive,
A victim of my own insecurities.

The Human vampire

Into the velvet darkness of your night
Where shadows dance in a mournful sorrow,
I drown in an endless slumber without light,
With no hope of seeing tomorrow.

With the blood of your love, you consume me,
Strip me from my emotions, my longings,
Inhuman and bitter, I see myself becoming,
As you bestow on me your eternal misery.

In melancholy, I tread on others' dreams,
Take away their pain and their suffering,
In longing I take away their lives,
Stripping them from what I am deprived.

You cast me into the shadows of immortality,
Fragile and broken in anguish and despair,
For the life within me has faded away,
And darkness has become my getaway.

Awake ye demons

Shake this insurmountable mountain
And let the smoke inside it rise,
Split that rock into two divides
And let the decaying stones be revealed.

Under the heating rays of the sun,
Let thy mountain rot back to stone,
Destroy the fortress around this castle,
And let the monument breathe anew.

Cast away the armor of this soldier,
Let him unburdened and free roam,
Heavy is the wall, empty is the well,
When I call to lift the door,

When I come to soothe my thirst,
Devoid are the quarters of this lonesome castle,
And the stench around its walls is suffocating,

Rise ye demons from underground
Rebel for under the rubble ...

The river runs dry

The river runs dry inside this mountain high,
Flowing towards its fate, leaving its shelter behind,

Searching for the roots of the tree of life,
It Flows out of bounds, leaving the well behind,

Finding in the unknown jewels flowing out,
The river runs through, stones falling out,

The cave's resounding sound echoes loud,
from its once youthful heart now blind,

And as the river runs dry, its rush fades with time,
Leaving the mountain empty, turning dry,

For the river runs dry within these eroding walls,
And the sun does not shine through its dusty holes,

But a drop of water is enough to shed a light,
Inside this darkened mountain, stripped from life,

Chained to the grounds, the mountain cannot move,
Longing for the river's flow, once so smooth,

The mountain rattles and crumbles with age,
And on goes the river, flowing towards its fate.

I long to be free

Anchored by fear, I feel incomplete,
my life is stagnant, as I long to be free,

holding on to memories,
that I fear may disappear,
closing the walls around me,
I fear someone to come near,

I stand still repeatedly
digesting an idea
yet I fear the outcome to be
less than what I dream.

I call out a name
with confusion and need,
but with doubts bred by fear,
I quickly retreat.

I speak of friendship,
yet have no one near,
for sharing and caring,
are nemesis to my fear.

In hopes I remain still,
chained by my fears,
the lacking I have felt
increases with the years.

The walls around me tighten
as I hope they crumble,
the cold within me has frozen
unable to truly feel.

I stand on the mountain,
ready for a new leap
and still my heart ponders
what journey lies beneath.

Anchored by my fears,
I cannot breathe
I am death within this life,
and I long to be free.

The Philosopher's hell

The philosopher in me is confused,
the poet within is tormented,
the lover inside me is divided,
the soul within is shaken,

The heart that beats is broken,
the mind that thinks reminisces,
the beauty inside was seized,
the warmth outside has ceased,

The promise within is silent,
the hope inside has faded,
the light has been extinguished,
the dream at night haunts the morning,

In wakefulness I am in a dream,
in sleep, I feel vividly the dream,
my nights are sleepless, turning to days,
my days are nights,
missing you in many ways.

Another love song I write,
over and again,
in contradiction, of thought
or feeling, again,

Of philosophy,
I have kept the complexity
of unresolved matters and mysteries,

Of poetry,
I have mastered the art of words,
creative and empty echoing back to me,

Of love,
I have learned the fear of pain;
the sweet taste it gives is sour in the end

The deadly kiss

The kiss of my rose became deadly
Its scent around me suffocating
Her image dwelt in my memory
Her breath on my lips intoxicating

Drowning in her arms in a sweet death
In agony I fight away the stench
A spreading disease from her fingertips
Laid like tears in the palm of my hands

Bittersweet is her sorrowful dance
A lingering sadness of a distant melody
A theatre of tragedy in a lamenting agony
A mournful song of deliverance

A hypnotizing spell you cast upon me
My fears and my pain disappear
In a decadent heaven of sins
In an ocean of betrayal and tears.

Prisoner of love

Why does my heart ache,
why does my soul weep,
when all is said and done
when all is lost and gone.
In sadness and in grief, it suffers in silence,
in despair and in sorrow, it clings to the pain.

Chorus: Mistress of the darkness or angel of despair
you've chained me, shamed me and abandoned me.
in oblivion I roam the earth
searching for you face at every turn.

You cast me in the shadows
behind locked and empty spaces
my eyes stray to find you near
my hands reach out to feel you

But in this misery I can tell you how I feel,
because you locked away the gates
that echo all my screams,
and however I call your name
Oh mistress you won't rescue me.

Chorus: Mistress of the darkness or angel of despair
you've chained me, shamed me and abandoned me.
in oblivion I roam the earth
searching for you face at every turn.

Deprived of hope, deprived of your love,
should I remain your prisoner,
or to other lands depart?

The devil's whisper

Oh hide thy vision and cover thine eyes,
For none but the devil stands before you now,
Deter thy sight from such monstrous vibes
Be not deceived by innocent eyes,

For none other is staring at you, dearest
but the mistress of darkness thou so fearst,
and thy smile dawning is but a lying trace
of the irony in thy heart and on thy face,

but the devil is not here to tempt thee again,
for thou hast proven before, thou hast failed,

let not thine ears be so sweetly betrayed
by nice compliments she hath once laid,
upon thy feet in a solemn swear
and upon thine lips in a bitter taste,

let not thy fury rage nor thine emotions
at what she hath once offered of devotion,
for the devil you knew hath changed its face
whence thou hast become an ancient phase,

so close thine eyes and move away
for the devil awaits another prey,
and paint not thy heart in black
for nothing can be gained back,

as thou hast clearly seen before
and spoken in words even more.

Mistress of the dark

Mistress of the dark
wearing your mask of grief,
your eyes betray you
showing your inner disease.

A flawless dream you seek,
in angels' hell sinks deep,
deceit drawn on your face,
signs of fear in every trace.

Hidden beneath your beauty
a rotten soul is lurking,
its crimes bear no guilt,
devoid of any feeling.

Daughter of eve, thou art not worthy,
thou hath forsaken and betrayed me,
but I forgive thee for I love thee,
hath said the Lord in his mercy.

But never again shall thou ask
for mine mercy in deviltry,
for mine wrath upon thee
shall be eternal misery.

RANDOM INSPIRATIONS

Seated woman in a painting

She sits by the hearth
contemplating the flames,
her own heat consuming
her desire as the fire burns,

And still she ponders
what has become of her long lost love
staring at his portrait
above the dancing flames,

She let go of her garment
that gently dropped at her sides,
as her eyes remained fixed
on the heat that burnt her eyes,

A single tear she shed,
that she could not withhold back,
as shivers ran down
all over her naked back.

She closed her eyes
and sighed briefly
choking with every new breath
that heaved her chest,

"Alas he is no longer
to witness my present predicament,
and I, in my lamentable state,
wish he could mend once again
the heart he has taken,
and that was willingly given,
to his grave"

87

*And gently sobbing,
she covered her face,
shivering at the thought
of his embrace;*

*his spirit will no longer be
confined to with her remain,
and without him, she fears,
life will never be the same.*

Winter in London

I see the sun bleeding in the sky
which out of mourning begins to cry,
thundering waves washing its tears away
as the dying sun finds a place to stay.

I hear the birds chanting in sadness
for lost is the spring in their fortress,
I hear them sing a song for the 'morrow,
for wherever the sun goes they will follow.

I see the earth sadly going in gloom,
flowers dying when still in bloom,
trees are shaking in the darkest cold
As they get stripped and quickly grow old.

I see the wind losing his temper,
raging through the fog in complete surrender,
swooshing motherless leaves away and astray
as the drums of winter begin to play.

The child within

When you figure out what you want out of life
You realize how incapable you are
Of achieving what you want,

When you're young,
opportunities knock on your door
Too hasty to choose,
You seldom open the right door

As time goes by, your body gets weary
Reality knocks you down,
Or illusions fill your mind,

Too blind, or too wise,
your choices narrow down
And the path you once dreamed of
Becomes far behind.

The image you once drew in your mind
When you were but a child
Full of dreams and life
Becomes a painting
out of focus in the sky

And as you look up trying to depict its meaning,
Clouds of uncertainty blind your eyes.

From there the dream is gone
As you try to carry on,
Then one day you realize
If only you were still a child.

Just Life

*L*ife is but a dream on the way to death, they say,
Love is just a game which justifies its destructive ends
The road we travel is but a bridge where both ends meet,
In a word nothing can be summed up without deficiency.

And aren't we all incomplete lacking something, in search of
another?
Isn't nature itself incomplete without the passing of all four
seasons?
Isn't earth fertile only with the seeds it has inhaled inside of
her,
For nothing else is whole except when its parts are assembled

And each particle by itself stands alone, useless in itself
Why, even the sky above finds in hell its compliment
And the angels which sing in laughter meet devils howling with
cries
And the sun that shines on a new dawn awaits the night to take
it away

And sailors who sail far away must wait for the tide to flow
their way
And will the sun ever set without the moon rising again?

Life must go on

Always on the run, facing yet another day,
unknown and unfamiliar is the road I take today.

With these dreams I hold, I seek better places,
leaving my prints in hearts soon without faces.

Is it regret, or a premature longing, my heart,
that you bear upon you before the journey starts?

For I can sense your grieving within me,
with each day that passes, your weakness betrays me.

I set adrift on the sea of pain again,
to reach my destination is my only gain

and farewell I bid you, yet with a glimpse of sadness,
for a part of you shall remain, eternally in this madness.

But not despair nor grief, will forestall my going,
and though I know how tired you are of running,

bereft and alone as you are, life must go on
for the time is ripe to finally move on.

Nothing here

Nothing binds me to this place any longer
My kin I have long abandoned yonder,

To places and faces I remain but a stranger
Perhaps a memory in the eyes of a painter,

The sun upon me wears its rays like flames,
With the rain a gloom reaches my heart with haste,

The land strips me from its bountiful richness,
Worse than a homeless, my dwelling is cold icicles.

There's nothing left that ties me to these memories
But a faint sting in the heart that will soon be fading,

time the instrument of perseverance, is but a partial healer,
when the heart goes astray, only pain grows deeper,

Through all these changes, my heart bleeds with longing,
Torn apart, forlorn, the holes inside it deepening,

A part of it remains in the dust after the storm,
With torn away promises and dreams long gone.

The Prince

In ancient Babylonian time
There, lived a prince with a crime
None other but the deed of love
Unto a maiden fair and deprived

From this obscenity arose his crime
As a gypsy tread on higher ground
Taking from a kingdom what is divine
What righteously was kept from older time

In bestowing kindly onto his lady
Who was recognized none but a gypsy
The prince shamed his title so inherited
And proved unfit to rule with merit

Cast out of his land and persecuted
The prince took refuge in lustful arms
As wine he drank and let down his arms
And captured by his army he was found

To renounce his title and save his land
The prince had no choice but one at hand
In a dark and silent night so blind
He killed his beloved to save his crown.

Black night and white light

*B*lack and white,

    darkness and light
without one

     there is no other
knowing one

    is knowing the other.

Through the blackest night

    shines strongest the brightest star
through the whitest snow

    a black dot is not so hard to find,

and yet nothing can be

    as dark or as white in itself
for together they make

    a painting unique in itself.

No angel of light

    is totally free of darkness
and the darkest angel

    craves in silence a glimmer of light.

White envies black

    for its shine under the sun
and black wishes to be pure

    as white in daylight.

A dark angel can only float

    so high far from the ground
in need of the wings of light

    to lift it higher where it can fly
a white angel can only sink

so low before it crashes on the ground
it needs the dark wings
                    to acknowledge the danger that lies.

Good without evil
                    is blinded to its deeds
evil without goodness
                    is pure destruction to all needs,

together they are strong,
                    in balance, in love
for love is the crib
                    that cradles their hearts,

black and white,
                    darkness and light
without one
                    there is no other to see the light.

Senses

Hear the whispering leaves
Greet the morning daylight,
Smell the fresh breeze
Trust the leaning trees
Swaying in the wind,
Humming in your ears.

Listen to the falling leaves
Brushing the earth as they heave,
Listen through the silence of the night,
Look at the stars shining bright.

Follow the moon glowing alight,
Seek the dream in the night,
Breathe the rainbow arching high,
See its colors in the morning rise.

Watch the sun setting high,
Feel its warmth in the sky,
Breathe the roses as you pass by,
Live the nature that is alive.

Climb the mountain without fear
It is smooth atop though steep,
Look the night right in the eye,
See the moon's smile, so shy.

See an image drawn in the clouds,
Grab it in a handful without doubts,
Inhale a breath of morning dew,
Taste its honey matched by few,
Give the morning a chance, anew.

Equilibrium
(Inspired by the movie)

*A*sk me not what it is I feel
When emptiness sucks me deep
Into its indifferent tyranny
Wearing her veil of misery.

A glimpse of death shrouded my vision
In the dark well I swarmed within,
A mermaid of changing colors appeared
From her breath, a gentle caress, released.

Shaken, I awoke from this slumber,
On my lips, a sweet taste remained,
I opened my eyes to the sound of thunder
And lighter had become my pain.

A longing sensation consumed my heart
That I felt pounding with a heavy start,
Tears invaded my eyes in a conscious attack,
I was feeling once again emotions I have lacked.

Said HE

*L*ook in the mirror, you will see
The true colors hiding underneath,
Look deep in the depth of your soul
You will find the answers you hold.

Look deep in the mirror and find
What others see behind your smile,
Look not in your heart for love
When shut from love its blind.

Look not for love with evil eyes,
When anger betrays what you hide,
Look not for love with regretful tears,
Love comes to you freely with the years.

Look not beyond what you cannot see,
Content yourself with what is real,
Look not for hope to restore your faith
But let your faith bring the hope you crave.

About the Author

Nadina Boun was born in Lebanon, studied in a French school and spent her time as a child traveling. She began writing poetry at the age of 14, though her style has changed and matured over the years, as she began broadening her writing into many genres such as short stories and plays mainly influenced by the classic French style.

Her first published book, *The Thinking Man, Paralysis by Analysis,* is a funny representation of rules in a man's head, a satirical account of our human nature set in the form of an analysis by none other than the thinking man.

Soon after, she released a play called *Le Duc*, in the French style of the dramatic plays, and is now pursuing her career in writing.

By the same author

The thinking man, paralysis by analysis
A satirical humor or rules in a man's hand, great coffee table read.

Le Duc
A one act play in the classic French style

Coming in 2012

The four letters of love
A collection of poems and short stories on love

From mysteries of the wind
A collection of the most recent poems in old style, and quotes

Made in the USA
Monee, IL
07 October 2024

67366268R00059